FINGERPICKING JAZZ FAVORITES

ISBN 978-1-4234-1657-9

HAL•LEONARD®
CORPORATION

7777 W. BLEUMOUND RD. P.O. BOX 13819 MILWAUKEE, WI 53213

Visit Hal Leonard Online at
www.halleonard.com

INTRODUCTION TO FINGERSTYLE GUITAR

Fingerstyle (a.k.a. fingerpicking) is a guitar technique that means you literally pick the strings with your right-hand fingers and thumb. This contrasts with the conventional technique of strumming and playing single notes with a pick (a.k.a. flatpicking). For fingerpicking, you can use any type of guitar: acoustic steel-string, nylon-string classical, or electric.

THE RIGHT HAND

The most common right-hand position is shown here.

Use a high wrist; arch your palm as if you were holding a ping-pong ball. Keep the thumb outside and away from the fingers, and let the fingers do the work rather than lifting your whole hand.

The thumb generally plucks the bottom strings with downstrokes on the left side of the thumb and thumbnail. The other fingers pluck the higher strings using upstrokes with the fleshy tip of the fingers and fingernails. The thumb and fingers should pluck one string per stroke and not brush over several strings.

Another picking option you may choose to use is called hybrid picking (a.k.a. plectrum-style fingerpicking). Here, the pick is usually held between the thumb and first finger, and the three remaining fingers are assigned to pluck the higher strings.

THE LEFT HAND

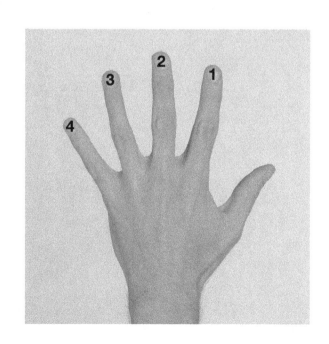

The left-hand fingers are numbered 1 through 4.

Be sure to keep your fingers arched, with each joint bent; if they flatten out across the strings, they will deaden the sound when you fingerpick. As a general rule, let the strings ring as long as possible when playing fingerstyle.

Bewitched

from PAL JOEY
Words by Lorenz Hart
Music by Richard Rodgers

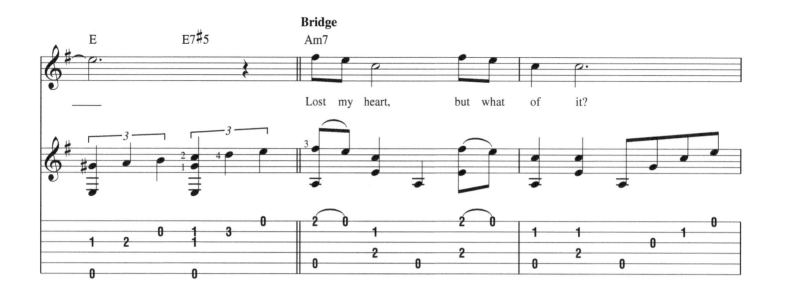

Bridge

E   E7#5   Am7

Lost my heart,   but what of it?

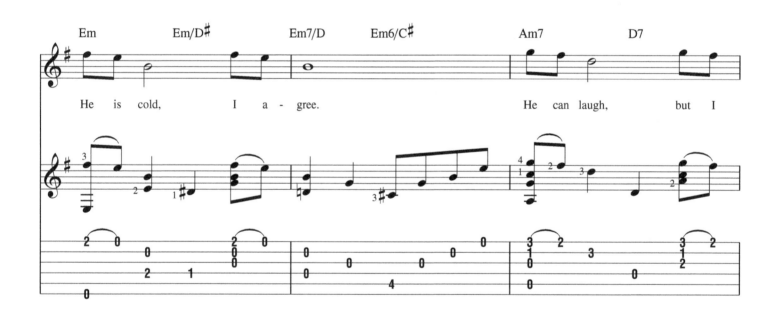

Em   Em/D#   Em7/D   Em6/C#   Am7   D7

He is cold,   I a - gree.   He can laugh,   but I

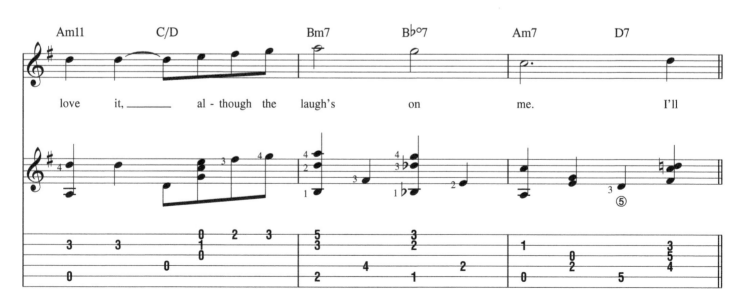

Am11   C/D   Bm7   Bb°7   Am7   D7

love it, _____ al - though the laugh's on me.   I'll

Outro-Verse

sing to him,   each spring, to him,   and   long for the day when I'll

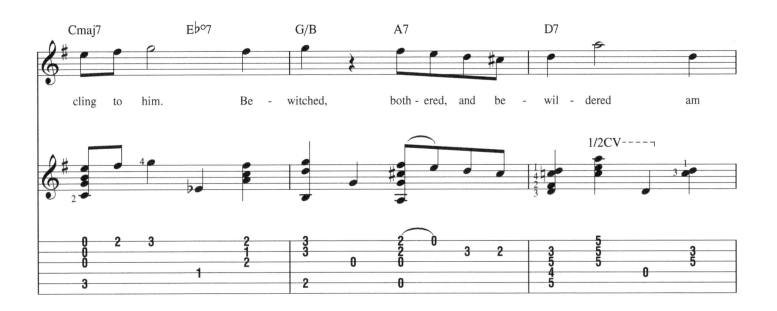

cling to him.   Be - witched,   both - ered, and be - wil - dered   am

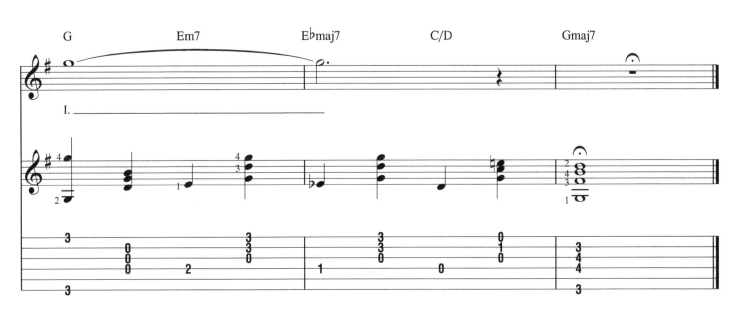

Blame It on My Youth

Words by Edward Heyman
Music by Oscar Levant

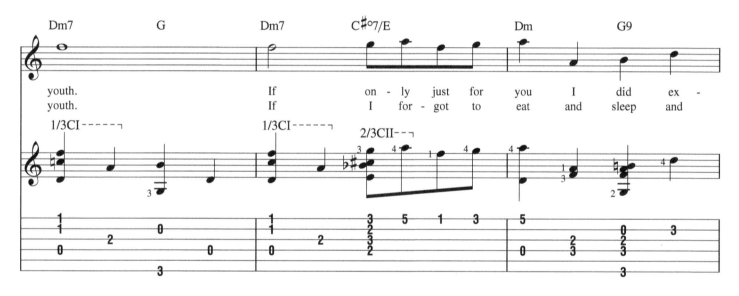

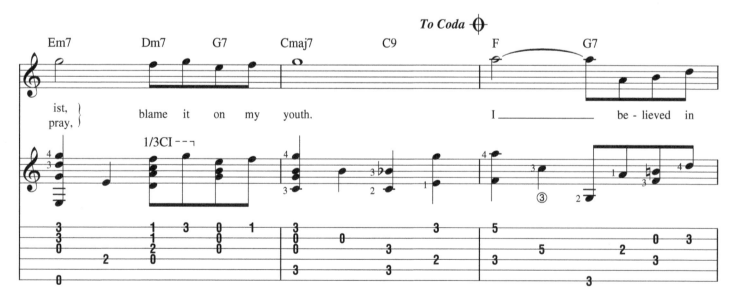

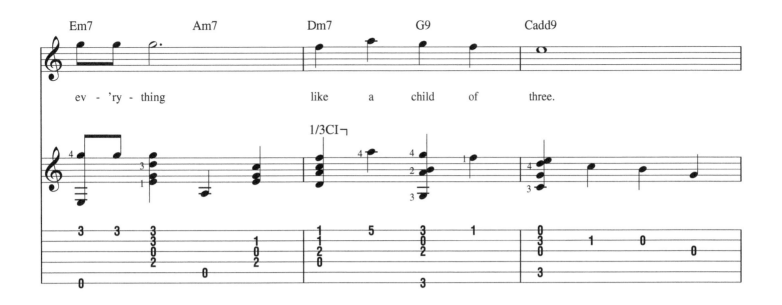

ev - 'ry - thing   like   a   child   of   three.

D.C. al Coda

You _____ meant   more   than   an - y - thing,   all   the   world   to   me!

⊕ Coda

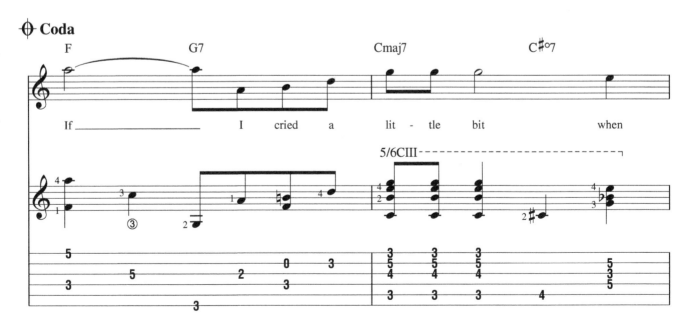

If _____   I   cried   a   lit - tle   bit   when

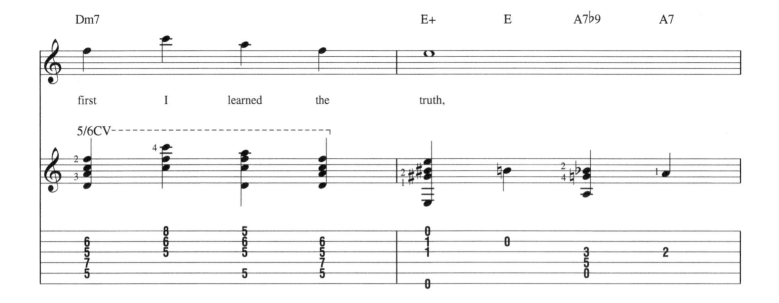

first I learned the truth,

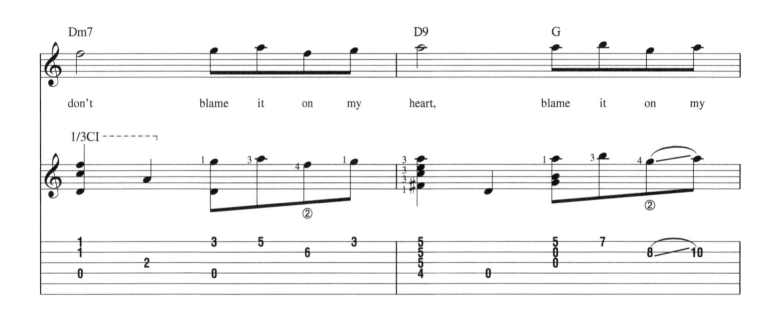

don't blame it on my heart, blame it on my

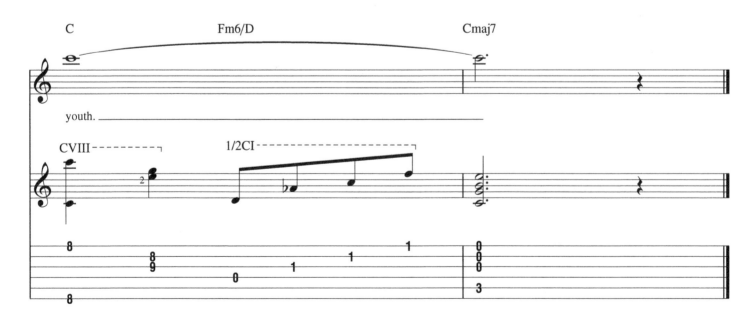

youth.

If I Should Lose You

from the Paramount Picture ROSE OF THE RANCHO
Words and Music by Leo Robin and Ralph Rainger

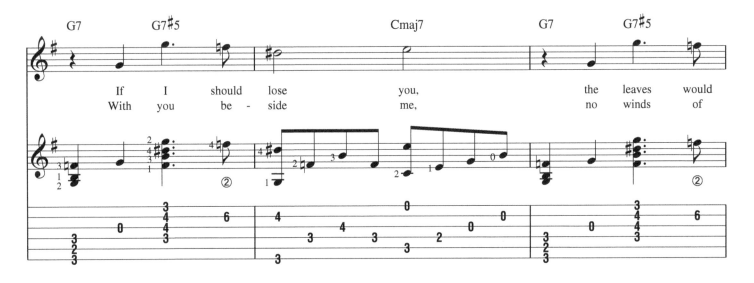

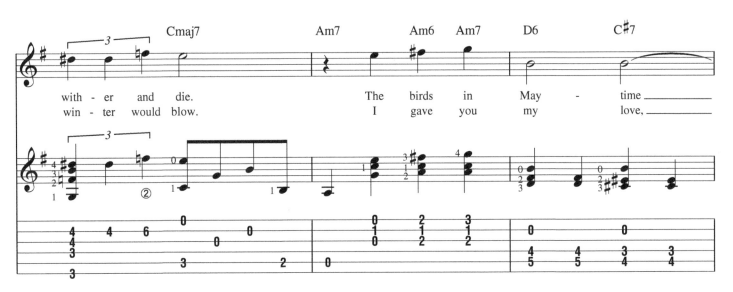

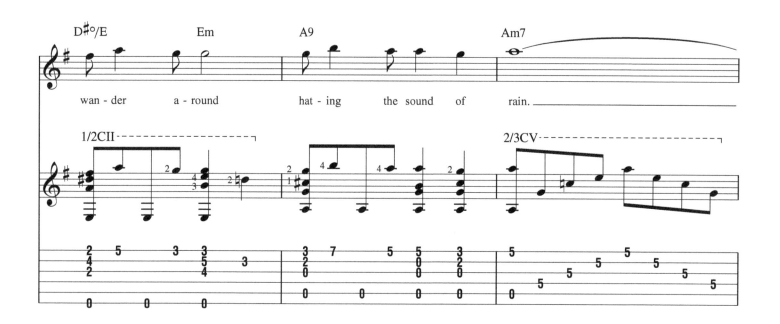

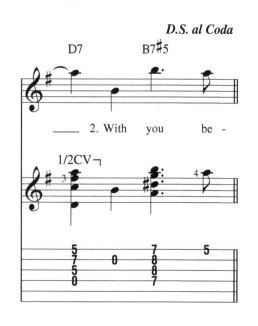

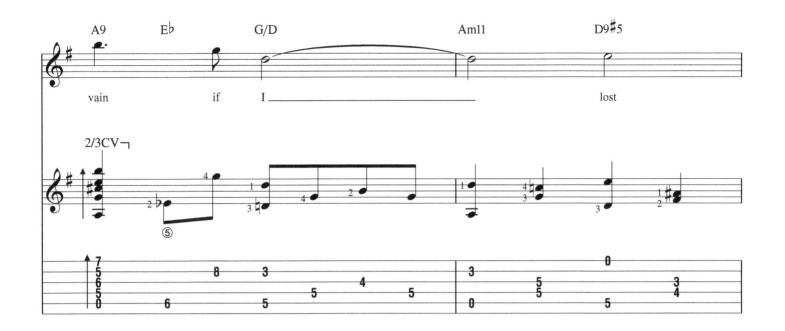

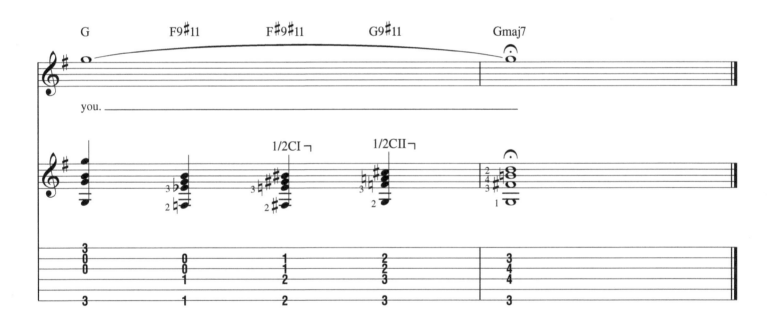

Cheek to Cheek

from the RKO Radio Motion Picture TOP HAT
Words and Music by Irving Berlin

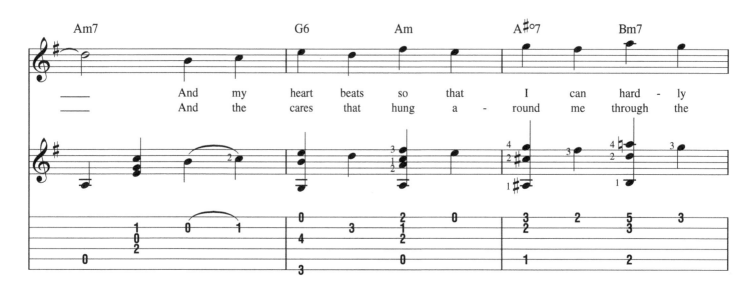

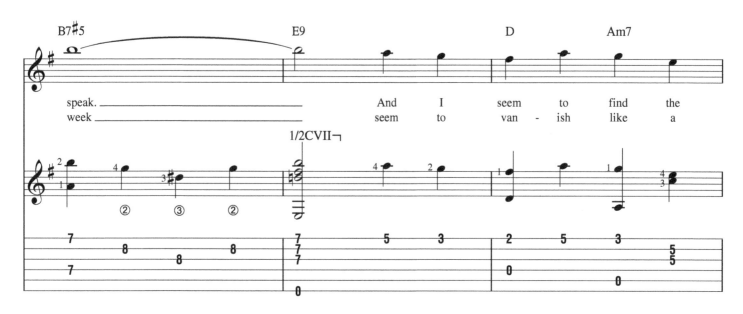

© Copyright 1935 by Irving Berlin
Copyright Renewed
This arrangement © Copyright 2013 by the Estate of Irving Berlin
International Copyright Secured   All Rights Reserved

hap - pi - ness I seek _____ when we're
gam - bler's luck - y streak _____

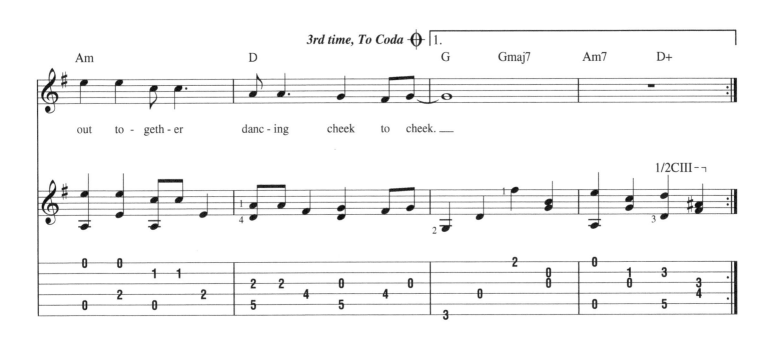

3rd time, To Coda ⊕ | 1.

out to - geth - er danc - ing cheek to cheek. __

1/2CIII

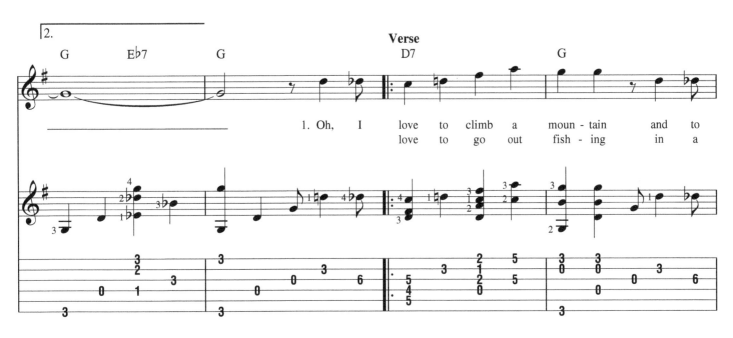

| 2.

Verse

_____ 1. Oh, I love to climb a moun - tain and to
love to go out fish - ing in a

reach the high - est peak, but it does - n't thrill me }
riv - er or a creek, but I don't en - joy it }

half as much ___ as danc - ing cheek to cheek. ___ 2. Oh, I

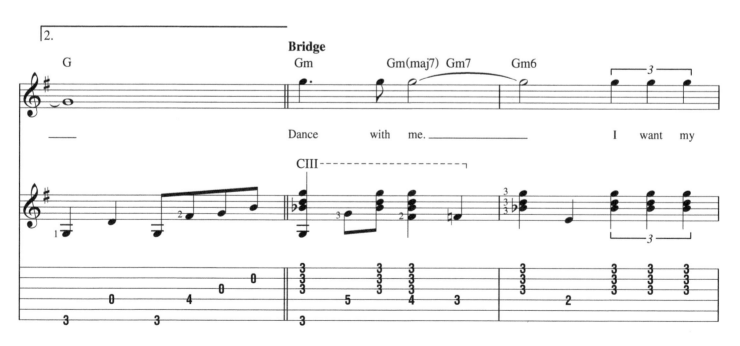

Bridge

___ Dance with me. ___ I want my

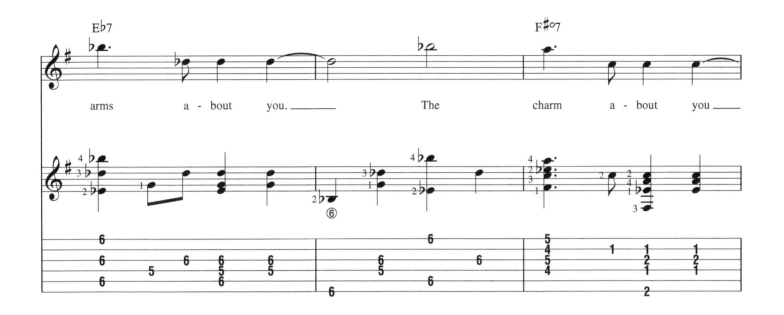

arms a - bout you._____ The charm a - bout you_____

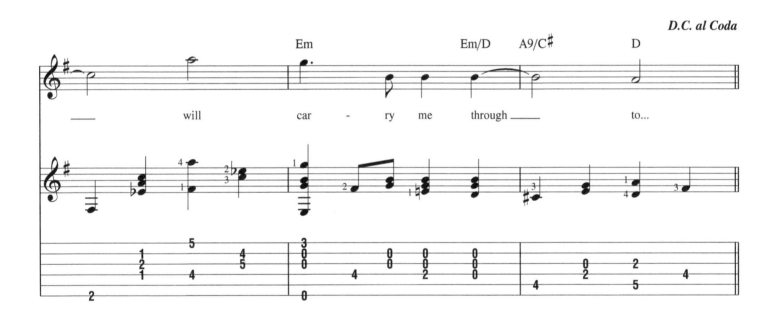

D.C. al Coda

_____ will car - ry me through_____ to...

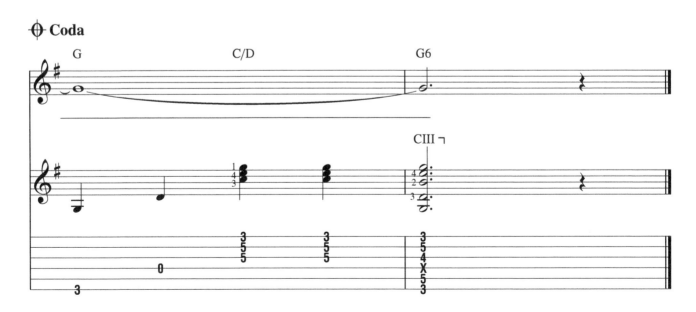

Coda

I'll Remember April

Words and Music by Pat Johnston, Don Raye and Gene De Paul

Drop D tuning:
(low to high) D-A-D-G-B-E

Verse
Moderately

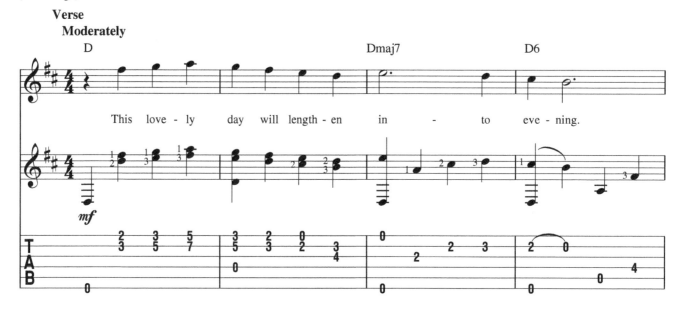

This love-ly day will length-en in - to eve - ning.

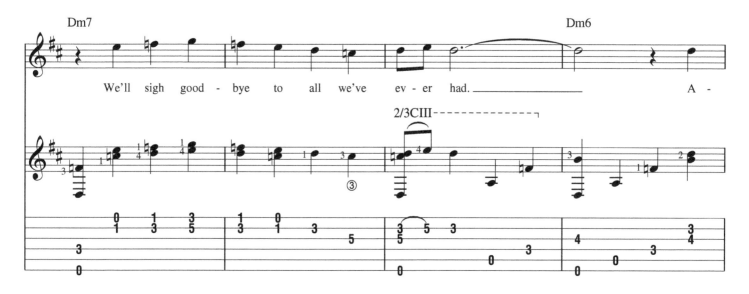

We'll sigh good - bye to all we've ev - er had. _____ A -

lone, where we have walked to - geth - er, _____ I'll re -

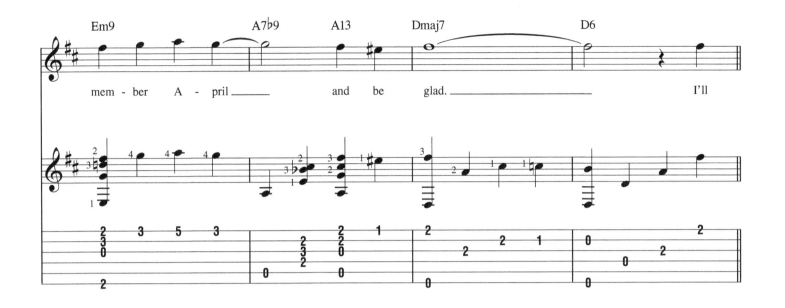

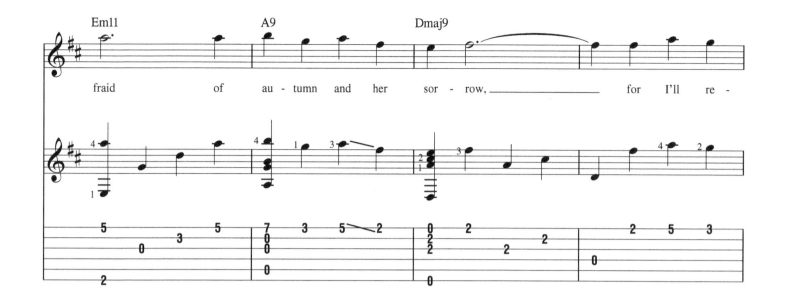

fraid of au - tumn and her sor - row,_____ for I'll re -

mem - ber _____ A - pril and you._____

Outro-Verse

The fire will dwin - dle in - to glow - ing ash - es,

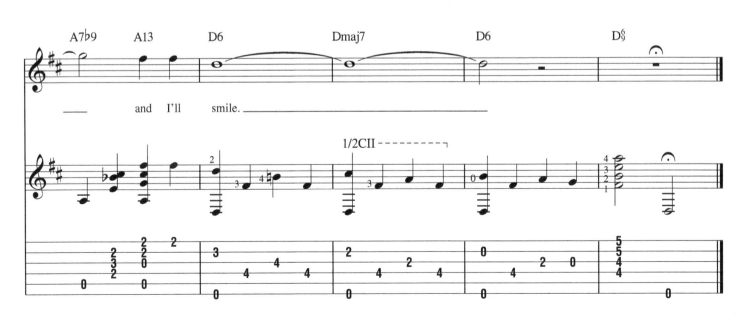

I've Got You Under My Skin

from BORN TO DANCE
Words and Music by Cole Porter

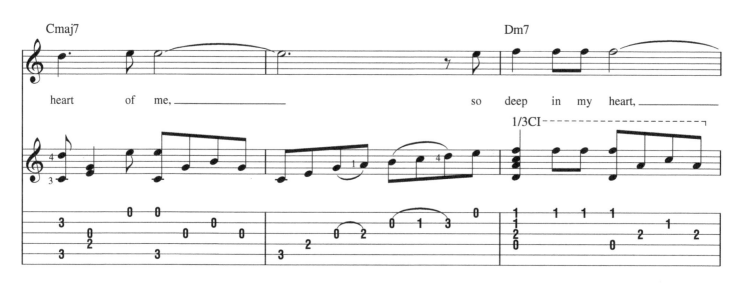

you're real - ly a part of me. _____ I've

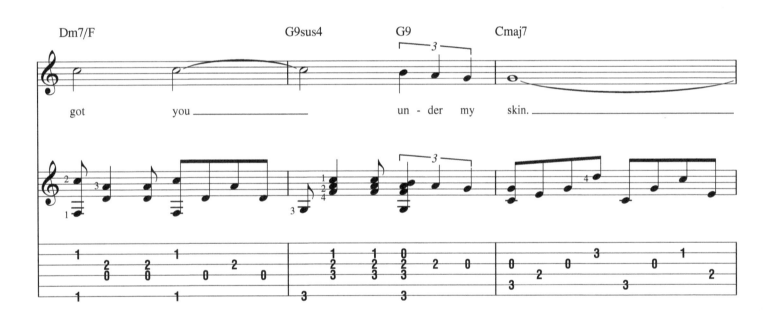

got you _____ un - der my skin. _____

Verse

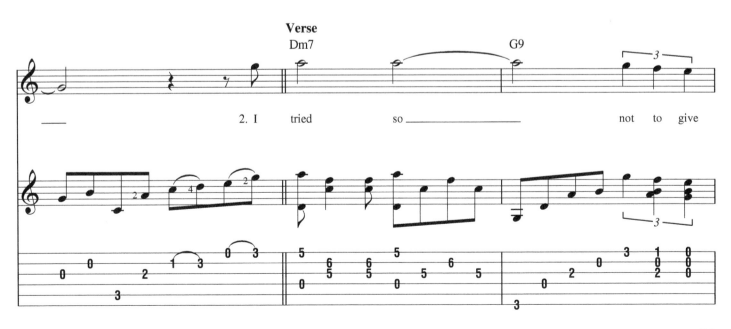

2. I tried so _____ not to give

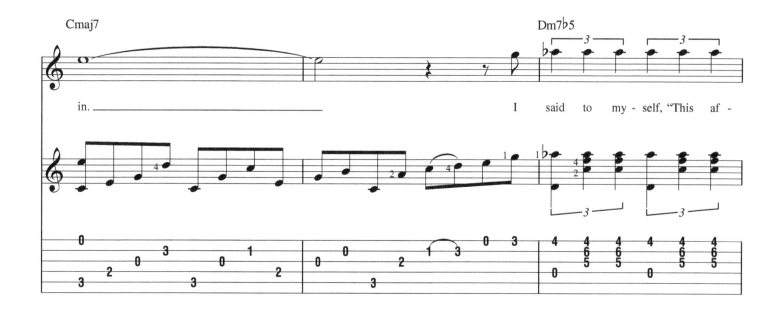

in. _____ I said to my-self, "This af-

fair nev - er will go so well." _____ But

why should I try to re - sist when, dar - ling, I know so well? _____

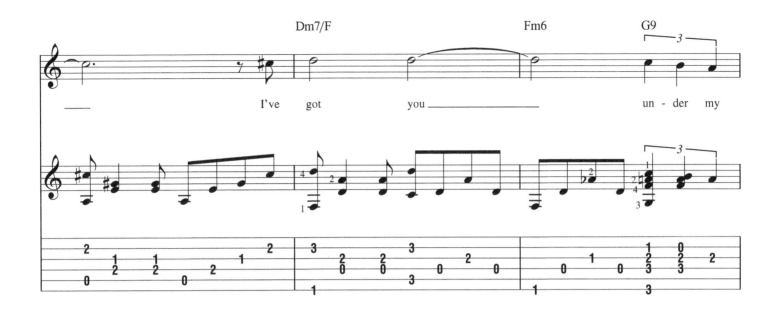

Dm7/F   Fm6   G9

I've got you _____ un - der my

Cmaj7   **Bridge**
                                         Dm7/F

skin. _____ I'd sac - ri - fice an - y - thing,

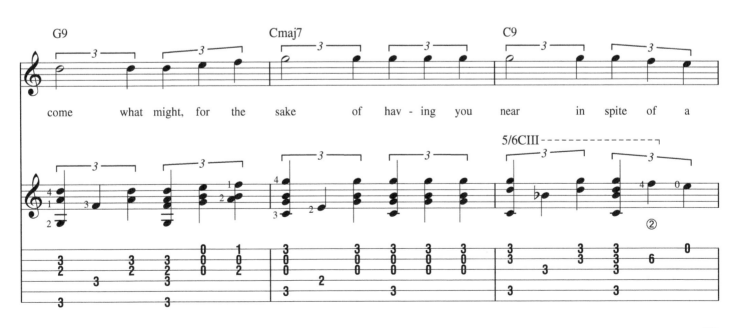

G9   Cmaj7   C9

come   what might, for the   sake   of hav - ing you   near   in spite of a

5/6CIII - - - - - - - - - - - - - - - -

②

warn - ing voice that comes in the night and re - peats and re - peats in my

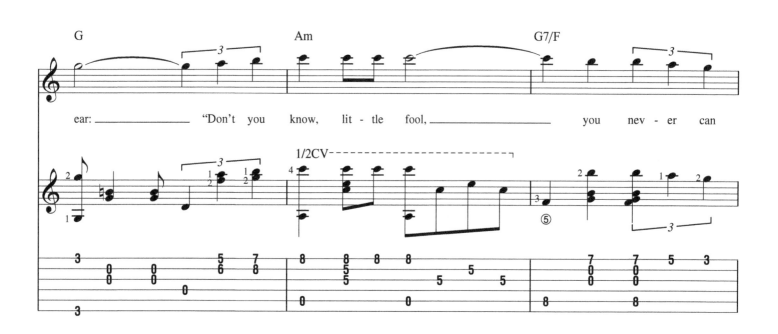

ear: _____ "Don't you know, lit - tle fool, _____ you nev - er can

win. _____ Use your men - tal - i - ty, _____

wake up to re-al-i-ty." But each

Outro

time I do, just the thought of you makes me stop be-fore I be-gin, 'cause I've

got you un-der my skin.

Isn't It Romantic?

from the Paramount Picture LOVE ME TONIGHT

Words by Lorenz Hart
Music by Richard Rodgers

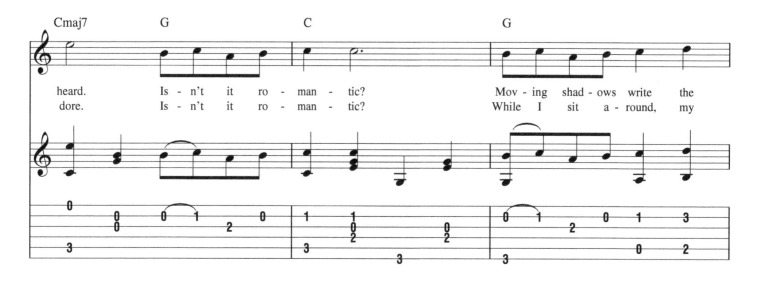

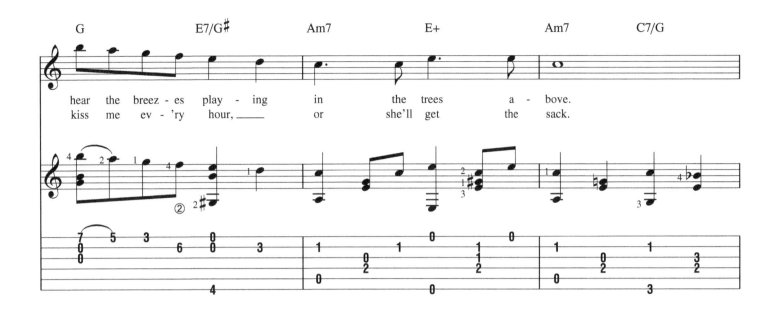

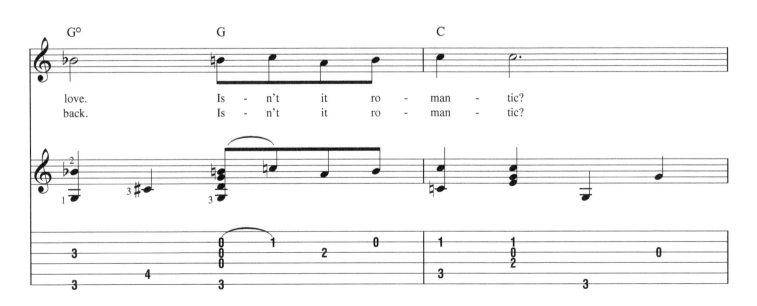

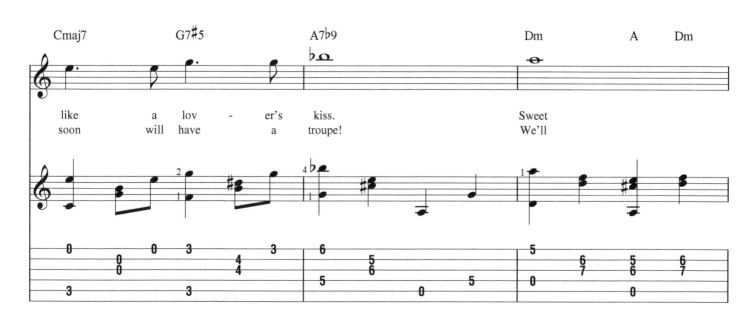

sym - bols in the moon - light, do you mean that I will fall in
help the pop - u - la - tion, it's a du - ty that we owe to

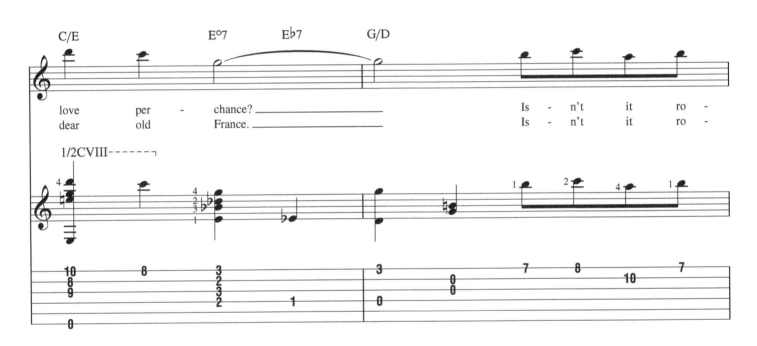

love per - chance?
dear old France.
Is - n't it ro -
Is - n't it ro -

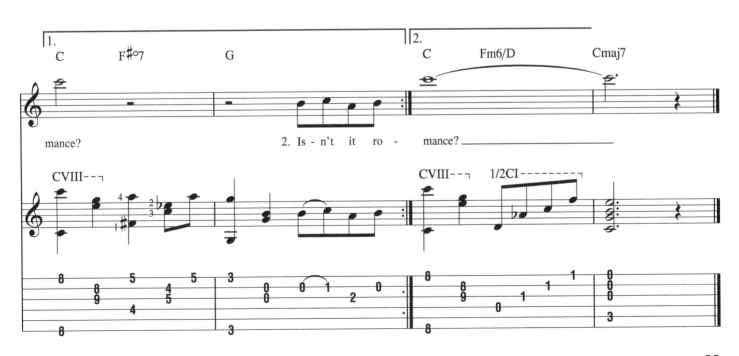

mance?
2. Is - n't it ro - mance?

Moonlight in Vermont

Words by John Blackburn
Music by Karl Suessdorf

Drop D tuning:
(low to high) D-A-D-G-B-E

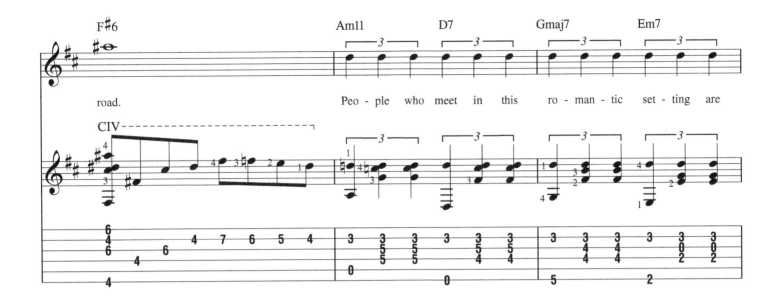

road.

Peo - ple who meet in this ro - man - tic set - ting are

D.C. al Coda

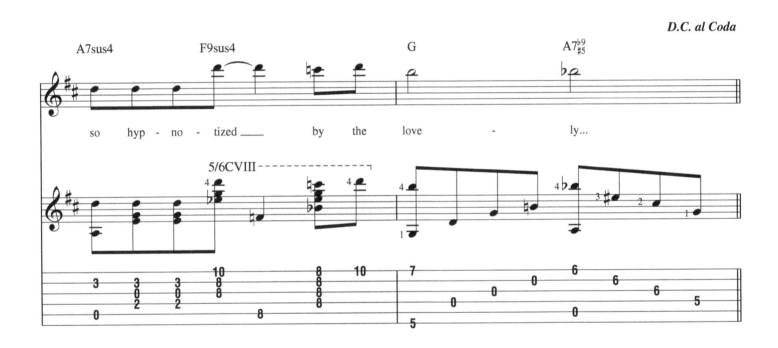

so hyp - no - tized ____ by the love - ly...

⊕ **Coda**

Outro

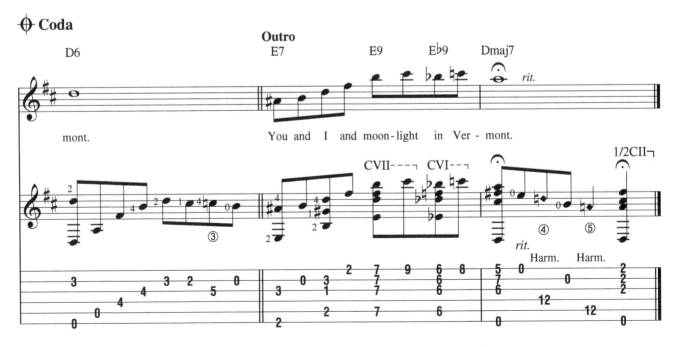

mont.

You and I and moon-light in Ver - mont.

My Heart Stood Still

from A CONNECTICUT YANKEE
Words by Lorenz Hart
Music by Richard Rodgers

Drop D tuning:
(low to high) D-A-D-G-B-E

Verse
Moderately

1. I took one look at you, that's all I
2. My feet could look step and walk, my lips could

meant to do and then my heart stood
move to and talk, and yet my heart stood

still! _____ still! _____ Though not a

Bridge

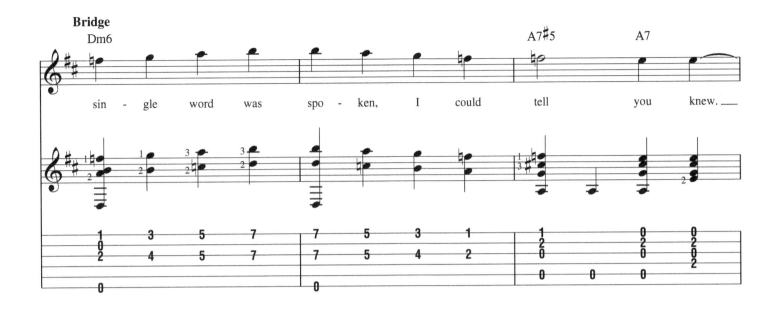

sin - gle word was spo - ken, I could tell you knew. ___

___ That un - felt clasp of hands ___

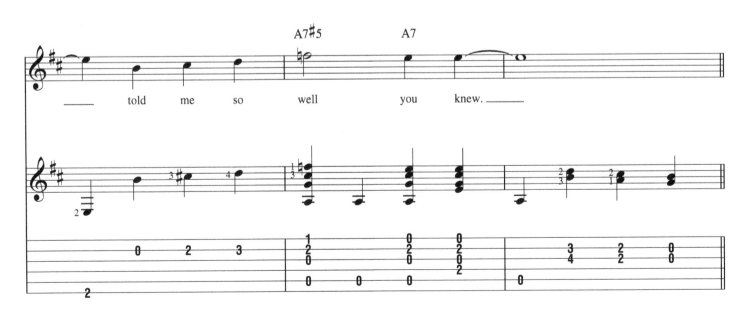

___ told me so well you knew. ___

Outro-Verse

I nev - er lived at all un - til the

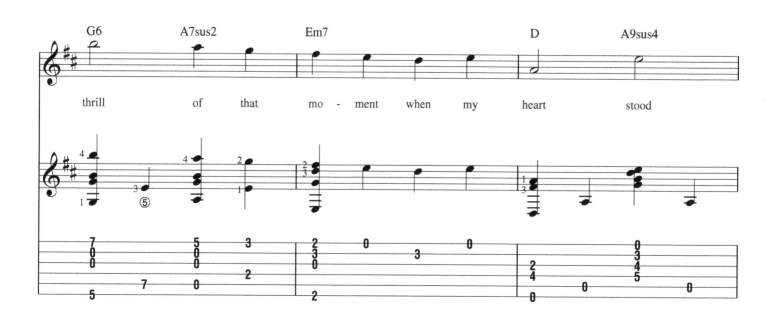

thrill of that mo - ment when my heart stood

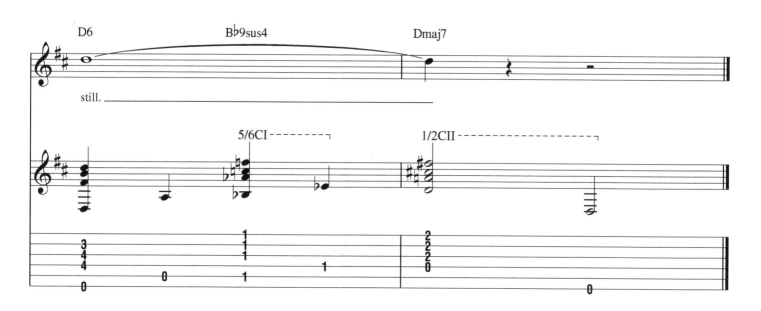

still.

Out of Nowhere

from the Paramount Picture DUDE RANCH

Words by Edward Heyman
Music by Johnny Green

Drop D tuning:
(low to high) D-A-D-G-B-E

Verse
Moderately

1. You came to me _____ from out of
2. If you should go _____ back to your

no - wbere. _____ You took my heart _____
no - wbere, _____ leav - ing me with _____

_____ and found it free. _____
_____ a mem - o - ry, _____

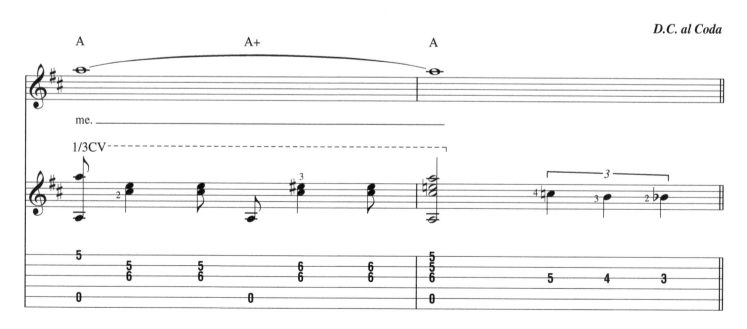

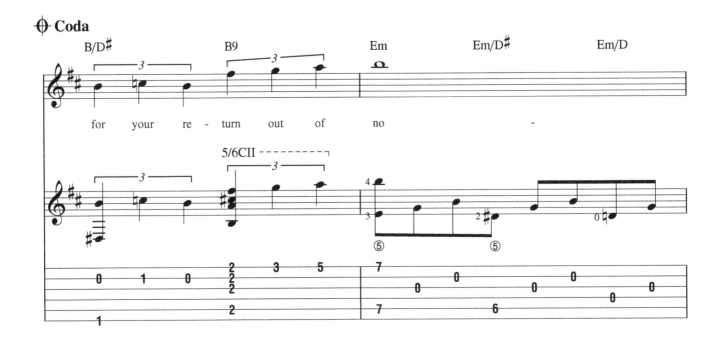

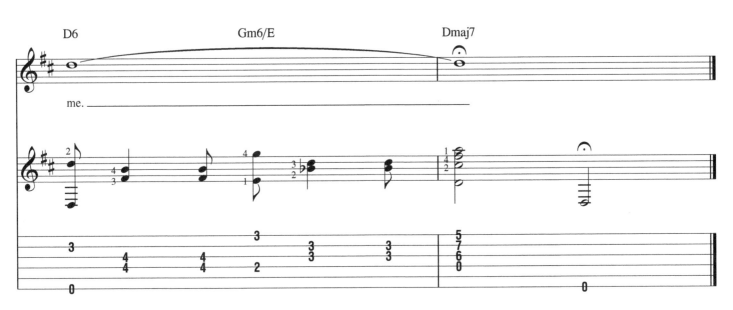

A Nightingale Sang in Berkeley Square

Lyric by Eric Maschwitz
Music by Manning Sherwin

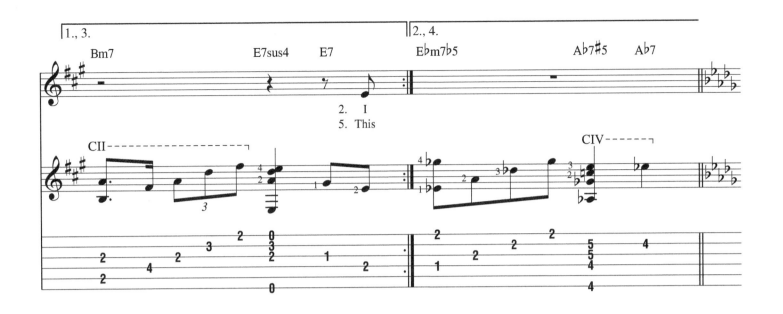

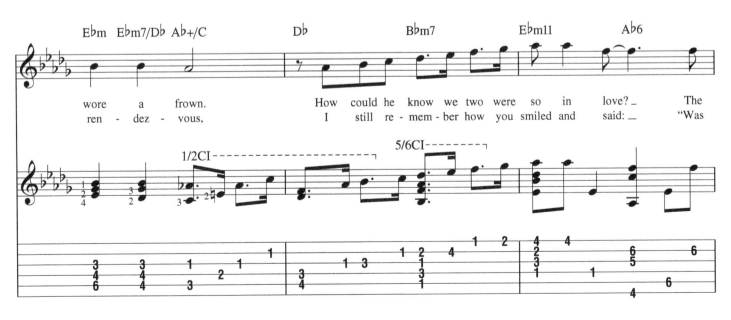

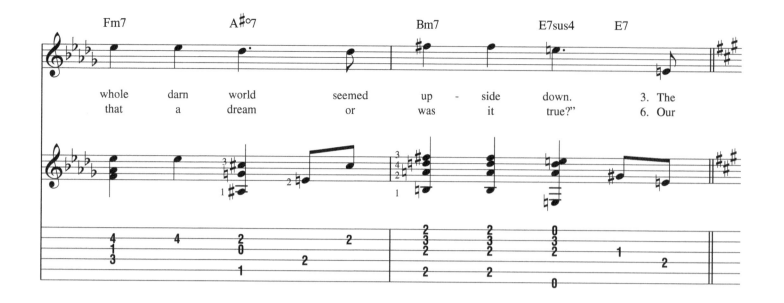

whole   darn   world   seemed   up - side   down.   3. The
that   a   dream   or   was   it   true?"   6. Our

Verse

streets   of   town   were   paved   with   stars.   It   was   such   a   ro - man - tic   af -
home - ward   step   was   just   as   light   as   the   tap - danc - ing   feet   of   As -

fair.   And   as   we   kissed   and   said,   "Good - night,"   a
taire.   And   like   an   ech - o   far   a - way,   a

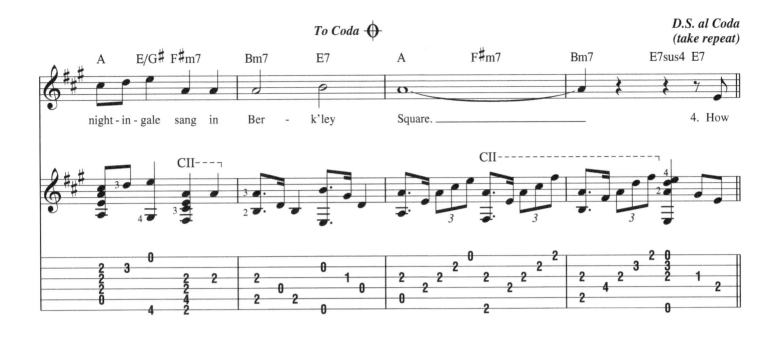

To Coda ⊕

D.S. al Coda *(take repeat)*

night-in-gale sang in Ber - k'ley Square. 4. How

⊕ **Coda**

Square. I know 'cause I was there,

that night in Ber - k'ley Square.

41

A Sunday Kind of Love

Words and Music by Louis Prima, Anita Nye Leonard, Stanley Rhodes and Barbara Belle

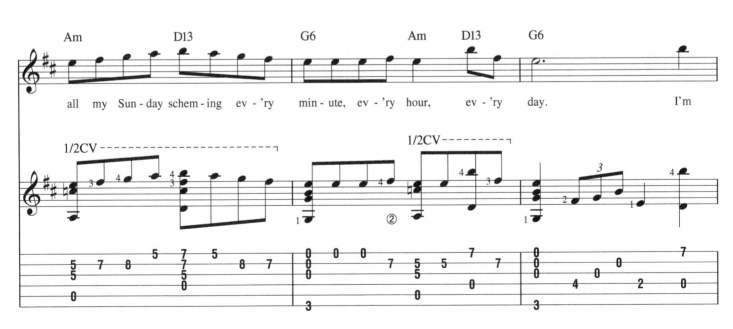

hop - ing   to   dis - cov - er   a   cer - tain   kind   of   lov - er

D.S. al Coda

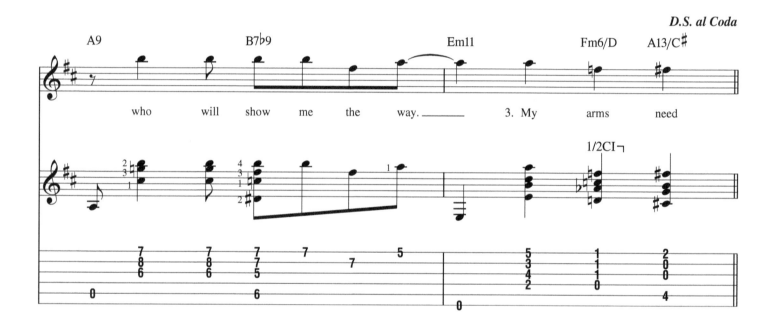

who   will   show   me   the   way._____ 3. My   arms   need

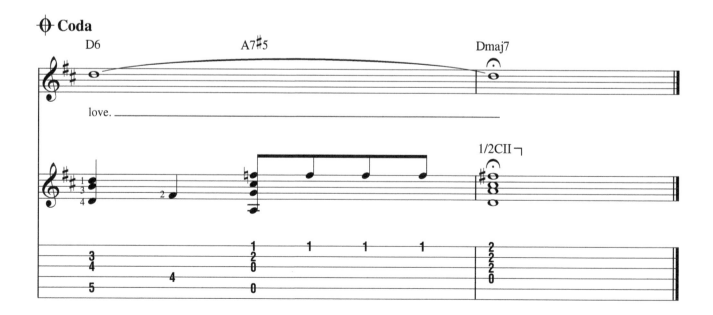

Coda

love. _____

Willow Weep for Me

Words and Music by Ann Ronell

Drop D tuning:
(low to high) D-A-D-G-B-E

Lis - ten   to   my   plea,   lis - ten, wil - low, and weep for   me. ___
Sad   as   I   can   be,   hear   me, wil - low, and weep for   me. ___
When the sha - dow falls,   bend, oh wil - low, and weep for   me. ___

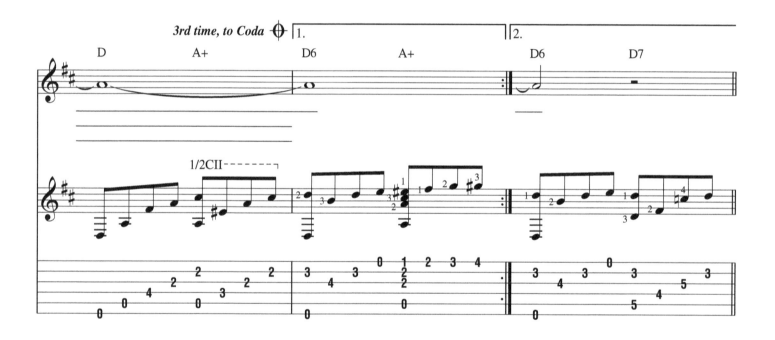

3rd time, to Coda

Whis - per   to   the   wind ___   and   say   that   love   has   sinned. ___   To

leave my heart a break-ing   and mak-ing a moan.__   Mur-mur to the night __   to

D.C. al Coda

hide her star-ry light, __   so   none will find me sigh-ing   and   cry-ing all a-lone. 3. Oh,

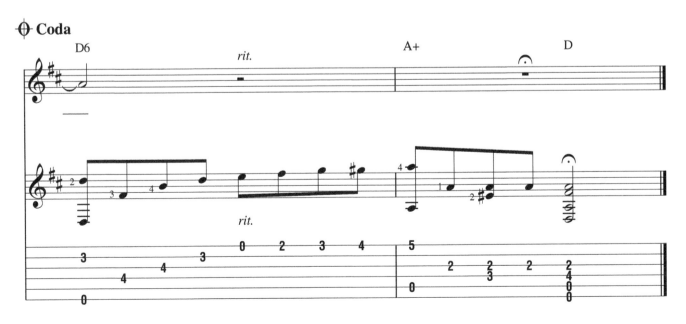

Coda

You Are Beautiful

from **FLOWER DRUM SONG**
Lyrics by Oscar Hammerstein II
Music by Richard Rodgers

Drop D tuning:
(low to high) D-A-D-G-B-E

Verse
Moderately

You are beau-ti-ful, small and shy.

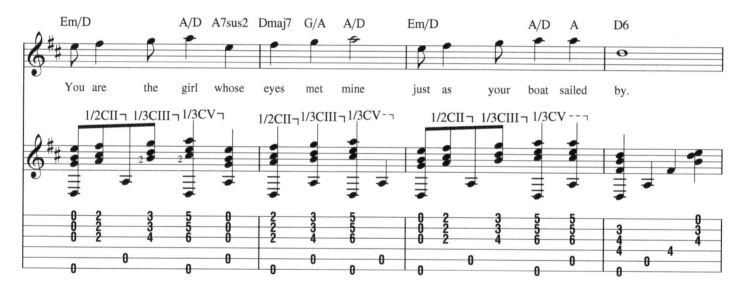

You are the girl whose eyes met mine just as your boat sailed by.

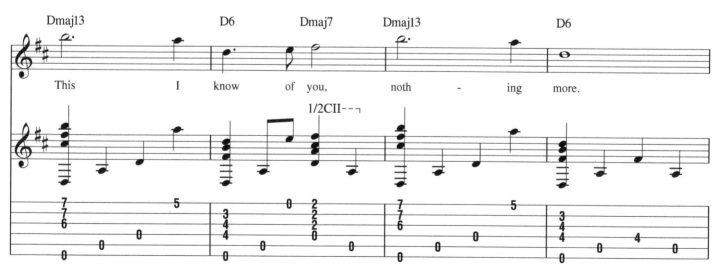

This I know of you, noth - ing more.

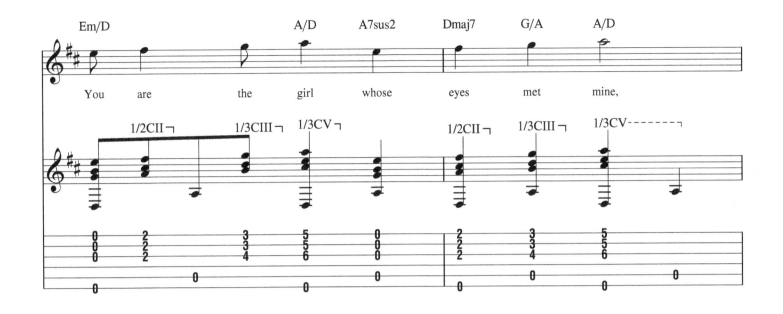

You are the girl whose eyes met mine,

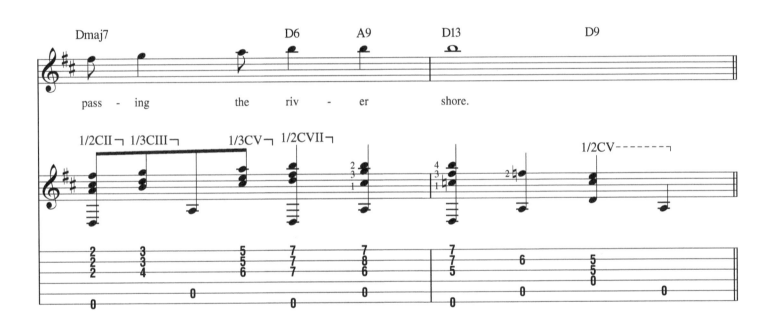

pass-ing the riv-er shore.

Bridge

You are the girl whose laugh I heard, sil-ver and soft and bright.

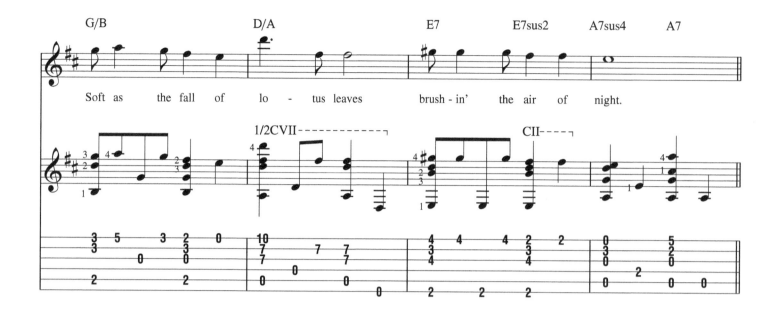

Soft as the fall of lo - tus leaves brush - in' the air of night.

Outro-Verse

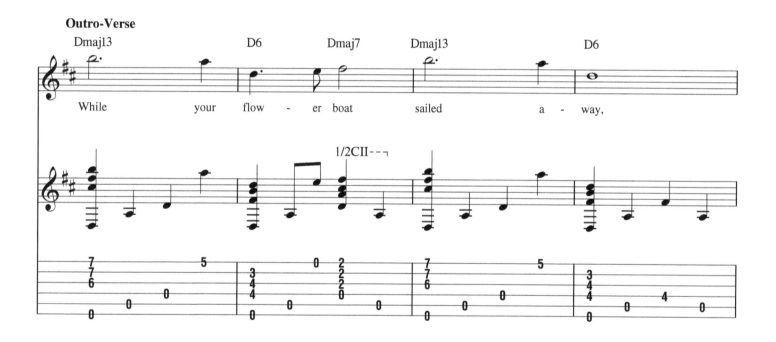

While your flow - er boat sailed a - way,

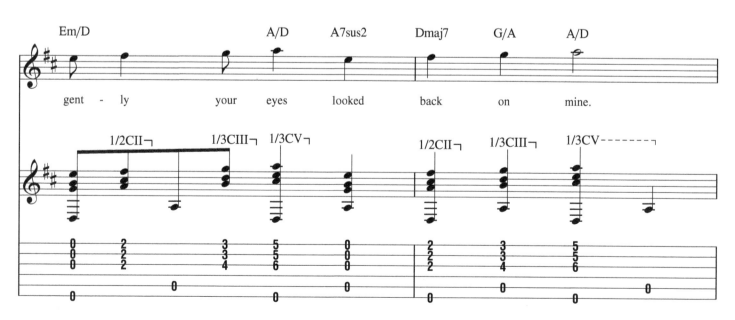

gent - ly your eyes looked back on mine.

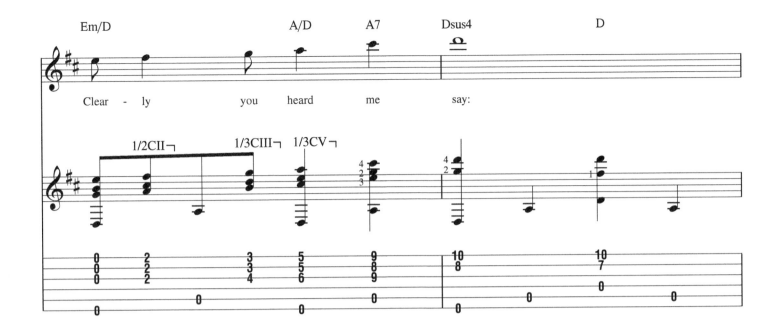

Clear - ly you heard me say:

"You are the girl I will love some -

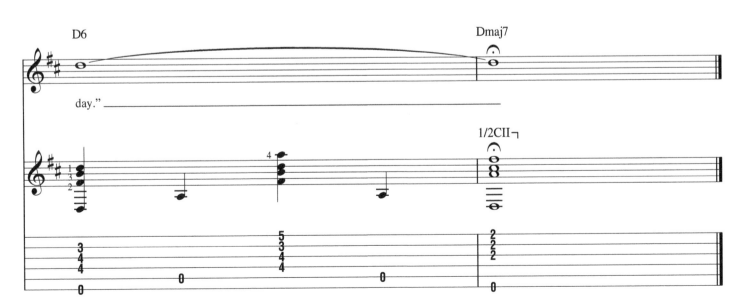

day." _____

You Don't Know What Love Is

Words and Music by Don Raye and Gene DePaul

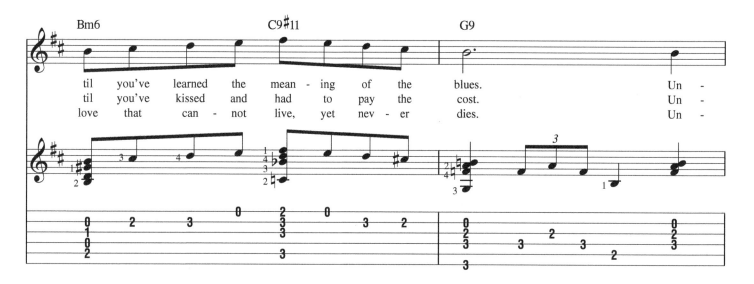

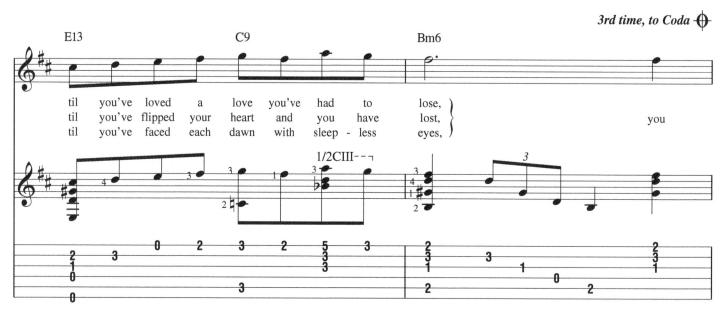

1.

G13   C#m7   F#7#5   F#7

don't   know _____ what   love   is. _____ 2.You

2.

G13   Gm6   Bm6

don't   know _____ what   love   is. _____ Do

Bridge

Em11   Eb7   Dmaj7   D6

you   know _____ how   a   lost   heart   fears ____ the

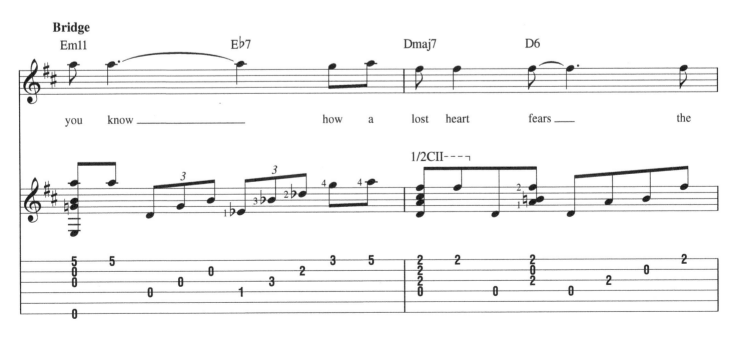

thought   of   rem - in - isc - ing? _____ And how   lips   that taste of   tears __

D.S. al Coda

_____   lose their   taste ___   for   kiss - ing? _____ 3. You

⊕ **Coda**

don't know _____ what   love is. _____

FINGERPICKING GUITAR BOOKS

Hone your fingerpicking skills with these great songbooks featuring solo guitar arrangements in standard notation and tablature. The arrangements in these books are carefully written for intermediate-level guitarists. Each song combines melody and harmony in one superb guitar fingerpicking arrangement. Each book also includes an introduction to basic fingerstyle guitar.

Fingerpicking Acoustic
00699614 15 songs......................$14.99

Fingerpicking Acoustic Classics
00160211 15 songs.......................$16.99

Fingerpicking Acoustic Hits
00160202 15 songs.......................$12.99

Fingerpicking Acoustic Rock
00699764 14 songs.......................$16.99

Fingerpicking Ballads
00699717 15 songs.......................$14.99

Fingerpicking Beatles
00699049 30 songs.......................$24.99

Fingerpicking Beethoven
00702390 15 pieces.....................$10.99

Fingerpicking Blues
00701277 15 songs $10.99

Fingerpicking Broadway Favorites
00699843 15 songs......................$9.99

Fingerpicking Broadway Hits
00699838 15 songs.........................$7.99

Fingerpicking Campfire
00275964 15 songs.......................$12.99

Fingerpicking Celtic Folk
00701148 15 songs......................$12.99

Fingerpicking Children's Songs
00699712 15 songs.........................$9.99

Fingerpicking Christian
00701076 15 songs.......................$12.99

Fingerpicking Christmas
00699599 20 carols.....................$10.99

Fingerpicking Christmas Classics
00701695 15 songs.........................$7.99

Fingerpicking Christmas Songs
00171333 15 songs.......................$10.99

Fingerpicking Classical
00699620 15 pieces......................$10.99

Fingerpicking Country
00699687 17 songs.......................$12.99

Fingerpicking Disney
00699711 15 songs.......................$16.99

Fingerpicking Early Jazz Standards
00276565 15 songs $12.99

Fingerpicking Duke Ellington
00699845 15 songs..........................$9.99

Fingerpicking Enya
00701161 15 songs.......................$16.99

Fingerpicking Film Score Music
00160143 15 songs.......................$12.99

Fingerpicking Gospel
00701059 15 songs.......................$9.99

Fingerpicking Hit Songs
00160195 15 songs.......................$12.99

Fingerpicking Hymns
00699688 15 hymns $12.99

Fingerpicking Irish Songs
00701965 15 songs.......................$10.99

Fingerpicking Italian Songs
00159778 15 songs.......................$12.99

Fingerpicking Jazz Favorites
00699844 15 songs.......................$12.99

Fingerpicking Jazz Standards
00699840 15 songs.......................$12.99

Fingerpicking Elton John
00237495 15 songs.......................$14.99

Fingerpicking Latin Favorites
00699842 15 songs.......................$12.99

Fingerpicking Latin Standards
00699837 15 songs.......................$17.99

Fingerpicking Andrew Lloyd Webber
00699839 14 songs.......................$16.99

Fingerpicking Love Songs
00699841 15 songs.......................$14.99

Fingerpicking Love Standards
00699836 15 songs $9.99

Fingerpicking Lullabyes
00701276 16 songs........................$9.99

Fingerpicking Movie Music
00699919 15 songs.......................$14.99

Fingerpicking Mozart
00699794 15 pieces......................$10.99

Fingerpicking Pop
00699615 15 songs.......................$14.99

Fingerpicking Popular Hits
00139079 14 songs.......................$12.99

Fingerpicking Praise
00699714 15 songs.......................$14.99

Fingerpicking Rock
00699716 15 songs.......................$14.99

Fingerpicking Standards
00699613 17 songs.......................$14.99

Fingerpicking Wedding
00699637 15 songs.......................$10.99

Fingerpicking Worship
00700554 15 songs.......................$14.99

Fingerpicking Neil Young – Greatest Hits
00700134 16 songs.......................$16.99

Fingerpicking Yuletide
00699654 16 songs.......................$12.99

HAL•LEONARD®

Order these and more great publications from your favorite music retailer at
halleonard.com

Prices, contents and availability subject to change without notice.

0322
279

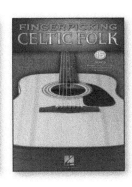

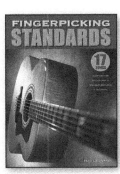

JAZZ GUITAR CHORD MELODY SOLOS

This series features chord melody arrangements in standard notation and tablature of songs for intermediate guitarists.

ALL-TIME STANDARDS

27 songs, including: All of Me • Bewitched • Come Fly with Me • A Fine Romance • Georgia on My Mind • How High the Moon • I'll Never Smile Again • I've Got You Under My Skin • It's De-Lovely • It's Only a Paper Moon • My Romance • Satin Doll • The Surrey with the Fringe on Top • Yesterdays • and more.
00699757 Solo Guitar...........................$16.99

IRVING BERLIN

27 songs, including: Alexander's Ragtime Band • Always • Blue Skies • Cheek to Cheek • Easter Parade • Happy Holiday • Heat Wave • How Deep Is the Ocean • Puttin' On the Ritz • Remember • They Say It's Wonderful • What'll I Do? • White Christmas • and more.
00700637 Solo Guitar...........................$14.99

CHRISTMAS CAROLS

26 songs, including: Auld Lang Syne • Away in a Manger • Deck the Hall • God Rest Ye Merry, Gentlemen • Good King Wenceslas • Here We Come A-Wassailing • It Came upon the Midnight Clear • Joy to the World • O Holy Night • O Little Town of Bethlehem • Silent Night • Toyland • We Three Kings of Orient Are • and more.
00701697 Solo Guitar $14.99

CHRISTMAS JAZZ

21 songs, including Auld Lang Syne • Baby, It's Cold Outside • Cool Yule • Have Yourself a Merry Little Christmas • I've Got My Love to Keep Me Warm • Mary, Did You Know? • Santa Baby • Sleigh Ride • White Christmas • Winter Wonderland • and more.
00171334 Solo Guitar $15.99

DISNEY SONGS

27 songs, including: Beauty and the Beast • Can You Feel the Love Tonight • Candle on the Water • Colors of the Wind • A Dream Is a Wish Your Heart Makes • Heigh-Ho • Some Day My Prince Will Come • Under the Sea • When You Wish upon a Star • A Whole New World (Aladdin's Theme) • Zip-A-Dee-Doo-Dah • and more.
00701902 Solo Guitar $14.99

DUKE ELLINGTON

25 songs, including: C-Jam Blues • Caravan • Do Nothin' Till You Hear from Me • Don't Get Around Much Anymore • I Got It Bad and That Ain't Good • I'm Just a Lucky So and So • In a Sentimental Mood • It Don't Mean a Thing (If It Ain't Got That Swing) • Mood Indigo • Perdido • Prelude to a Kiss • Satin Doll • and more.
00700636 Solo Guitar $14.99

FAVORITE STANDARDS

27 songs, including: All the Way • Autumn in New York • Blue Skies • Cheek to Cheek • Don't Get Around Much Anymore • How Deep Is the Ocean • I'll Be Seeing You • Isn't It Romantic? • It Could Happen to You • The Lady Is a Tramp • Moon River • Speak Low • Take the "A" Train • Willow Weep for Me • Witchcraft • and more.
00699756 Solo Guitar..........................$17.99

JAZZ BALLADS

27 songs, including: Body and Soul • Darn That Dream • Easy to Love (You'd Be So Easy to Love) • Here's That Rainy Day • In a Sentimental Mood • Misty • My Foolish Heart • My Funny Valentine • The Nearness of You • Stella by Starlight • Time After Time • The Way You Look Tonight • When Sunny Gets Blue • and more.
00699755 Solo Guitar..........................$16.99

LATIN STANDARDS

27 Latin favorites, including: Água De Beber (Water to Drink) • Desafinado • The Girl from Ipanema • How Insensitive (Insensatez) • Little Boat • Meditation • One Note Samba (Samba De Uma Nota So) • Poinciana • Quiet Nights of Quiet Stars • Samba De Orfeu • So Nice (Summer Samba) • Wave • and more.
00699754 Solo Guitar..........................$16.99

Order online at **halleonard.com**

HAL•LEONARD®